About the Author

Bertil Ravald has been the professional masseur for Sweden's top soccer club, Malmö FF, for eighteen years, as well as the masseur to such international sports stars as Björn Borg, Mats Wilander, and Pelé. He has also been the Swedish team masseur for the European Championships and Olympics and trainer for the Swedish javelin and shot-put teams.

Professor Nils E. Westlin, Doctor of Medicine at Malmö General Hospital's Orthopedic Clinic, writes: "Ravald's special interest in sports injuries extends over thirty-five years, during which time he has held innumerable courses on sports and massage, written textbooks on sports injuries and, with unflagging enthusiasm, developed the potential of massage in the treatment of muscular pain. With clearly illustrated, easy-to-follow instructions, Bertil Ravald shares with the reader the special massage techniques he has developed over the years."

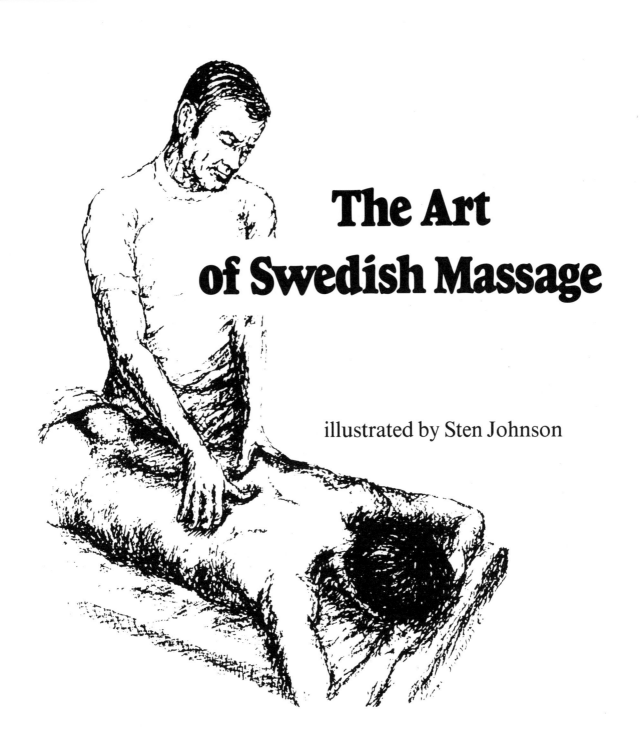

The Art of Swedish Massage

illustrated by Sten Johnson

The Bergh Publishing Group, Inc.
USA – Switzerland – Sweden – Spain

Copyright © 1982 by Edition Sven Erik Bergh in EUROPABUCH AG.,
6314 Unterägeri, Switzerland
First United States edition 1985 by
The Bergh Publishing Group, Inc., New York, N. Y. 10016
c/o E. P. Dutton Inc., 2 Park Avenue,
Telephone: (212) 725-1818.

ISBN 0-930267-03-6
All rights reserved. Except for use in a review, the reproduction or utilization of this work in any form or by
any electronic, mechanical, or other means, now known or hereafter invented, including xerography,
photocopying, and recording, and in any information storage and retrieval system is forbidden without the
written permission of the publisher.
Originally published by Edition Sven Erik Bergh, in der Europabuch AG, Unterägeri, Switzerland,
under the title of *Massage: Ein Handbuch für Jedermann*
Printed in Germany
Mohndruck Graphische Betriebe GmbH, Gütersloh

Contents

Note to the Reader	7
The Massage Environment	9
What is Massage?	10
Some Massage Do's and Don't's	11
The Four Basic Techniques	12
Effleurage	12
Friction	12
Petrissage	13
Tapotement	13
Special Equipment	14
Massaging Different Muscle Groups	15
feet	17
shins (front)	29
shins (back)	30
thighs (front)	39
thighs (back)	49
hips	57
back	63
shoulders	75
neck	83
forearm extensors	89
forearm flexors	90
upper arms (front)	97
upper arms (back)	98
stomach	103
chest	109
Some Final Tips	115

Note to the Reader

This massage handbook is intended for use by athletes and non-athletes alike. No prior knowledge of anatomy is needed; the instructions and accompanying diagrams have been specially designed with the general reader in mind. Massage for each section of the body is described in turn and, wherever possible, the action of the muscle groups has been explained.

It is suggested that readers wishing to extend their knowledge of massage even further consult some of the many books available on the functioning of muscles and joints. In this way, a greater understanding of the basic techniques can be reached.

THE ART OF SWEDISH MASSAGE has been richly illustrated with detailed drawings of the massage techniques appropriate to each group of muscles. After a little practice, you, too, can use massage to prevent injury and ease strained muscles—your own as well as those of your friends.

Good luck!

Bertil Ravald

The Massage Environment

A massage can be given at home on a couch or chaise longue if no massage table is available. To avoid irritation of the hair follicles, a high-quality liniment or massage ointment should be used. It is important for the masseur that the skin be smooth and supple. A massage can take anywhere from 15 minutes to 1 hour and a shower is recommended afterwards. If there are no shower facilities available, the liniment or ointment can be removed with a damp towel or paper towels. Locker rooms should be equipped with a massage table, which stands about $2\frac{1}{2}$ feet high and 2 feet wide. The table is covered with a paper sheet which is changed after each treatment. If the massage takes place before a training-session or competition, the liniment or ointment need not be removed until the individual showers after the work-out or game.

Masseurs should wash their hands and scrub their nails before and after each treatment. Cleanliness is of the greatest importance! So, too, are the clothes worn by the masseur when at work: a tracksuit and comfortable shoes are most suitable. Professional masseurs maintain very high standards which may be difficult to duplicate in the home. But, no matter where a massage is given, every effort should be made to keep the massage environment clean and tidy. What the amateur masseur *must* have are: soap and water, liniment or ointment, clean hands and manicured nails, plus practice, practice and more practice in the art of massage.

What is Massage?

Massage is an ancient form of therapy, used by the Greeks more than 4000 years ago to cure a variety of illnesses. They also used it to prepare their athletes for the olympics and other major sporting contests.

Today's athletes are still in need of massage. One point must be made clear from the outset—massage *cannot* cure inflamed or damaged muscles or joints. But massage *can* ease stiff, tense muscles which, if left untreated, can lead to problems like lumbago and chronic shoulder and neck trouble. Athletes and fitness enthusiasts will therefore find this handbook of great value. Despite the widespread use of massage, little literature exists giving step-by-step instructions in massage technique. After 30 years' experience as masseur and sports instructor, I hope to pass on some of my knowledge to other sports enthusiasts. I know that massage can often be of great benefit, chiefly in preventing such sports injuries as muscle ruptures.

During my 19 years at Malmö's soccer club, we seldom had a case of muscle rupture. This has convinced me of the importance of massage before every training session and game. Anyone who is actively engaged in sports or exercise of any sort needs massage to keep the muscles free from waste products and to relieve stiffness. Massage increases the rate of circulation in the blood and lymphatic systems, allowing the muscles to absorb more oxygen and work harder. Massage strengthens and tones the muscles while creating an overall feeling of physical well-being which is reflected in an athletes performance during a training session or competition. We often hear that athletes who are used to receiving a massage before a work-out or game find they cannot do without it. This certainly proves the importance of massage. An understanding of massage and its contribution to keeping the body in good shape is an important part of any athlete's training.

The value of massage is currently the subject of scientific testing. In those countries where the importance of massage is already understood, national teams are invariably accompanied by one or two masseurs during international competitions or tours. However, it is not only athletes who benefit from massage. In some sense, all of life is a work-out. Muscle strain is the result of poor posture, repetitive movements and the stress of day-to-day life. Housewives experience muscle and back strain as they stand and lift and carry home several tons of food from the supermarket each year.

Nine out of ten of us have at some time experienced the discomfort of backache. Here, too, massage can help. However, a slipped disc (fortunately, a much less common ailment) should not be treated by a masseur, but left to doctors and physiotherapists.

We must not exaggerate the potential of massage—it is not a cure-all. But it is a way of learning about our muscles and how they work and with this knowledge we can help ourselves and our friends.

Some Massage Do's and Don't's

Most muscles can be massaged. At first it is best to practice on someone close to you who can let you know just how firmly you should use your hands when massaging. This way you will soon learn the amount of pressure you need to exert in order for the massage to be effective. A massage session should last between 15 minutes and an hour to be truly beneficial.

Only muscles should be massaged. Joints, tendons and glands should be avoided, since they have a poor blood supply and can easily become irritated or even inflamed. My advice therefore to beginners is to stick to the muscles. However, inflamed, swollen or bruised muscles should never be massaged. Bruises should be left alone for 10—12 days after they occur, since massaging involves the risk of spreading the stagnant blood into the surrounding area. All injuries *must* be allowed to heal before you start massaging them.

In team sports such as football, soccer, handball and ice hockey, aggressive tackling with the knee or foot can result in heavy bruising of the thigh. Many inexpert masseurs try to eliminate this bruising by massage, without success. Such major bruising should be treated like a rupture and allowed to heal for ten to twelve days. Get yourself a book on sports injuries and learn to identify them and always ask the advice of a doctor or other expert when in doubt! The masseur must always be on guard when massaging an injured athlete. Fortunately, many doctors now take a special interest in sports injuries. By following a doctor's advice, you can avoid causing injury by massage. At the same time you can learn an enormous amount from someone who has studied the human body in great detail.

The Four Basic Techniques

Although individual masseurs use different methods, they all share certain basic techniques. It is important to note before starting that greater pressure is used in sports massage than in the treatment given by a physiotherapist to a sick patient. The massage described in this handbook is intended for healthy individuals.

The four basic techniques
Effleurage = stroking
Friction   = rubbing
Petrissage = kneading
Tapotement = shaking and vibration

Effleurage
Stroking is the form of massage used at the beginning of a session at the same time the liniment or ointment is applied. The masseur adapts his hand or hands to the part of the body he is massaging. The strokes can be short or run the full length of the muscle and should be made rhythmically and without interruption. The masseur's hands maintain body contact all the time. Each massage session begins and ends with massage and the strokes are always made in the direction of the heart. Having increased the circulation through the blood vessels and lymphatic system, we can move on to the next technique: friction.

Friction
Rubbing involves small circular movements performed by the thumbs or fingers. The palm of the hand can be used on larger sections of the body. Where the muscles are thick, the knuckles can be used, though care must be taken with muscular subjects not to press too hard.

Too much pressure can cause bruising and bleeding, for example, in the muscles of the buttocks. Not that this is in any way dangerous, but the results are ugly. Friction massage is given slowly, though at varying speeds. Alternate while working: first massage with the thumbs using the fingers for support, then massage with the fingers using the thumbs for support. On larger sections of the body, the palms of the hands can be used. Friction massage is ideal for massaging small areas, such as the hands and feet. The technique stimulates the circulation, activates the blood vessels and tones the striated (voluntary) muscles. This way, the muscles' ability to store oxygen is increased. When the friction massage has been completed, you can then continue with the heaviest technique: petrissage or kneading.

Petrissage
Kneading is the technique that beginners find most difficult to master, since there is, at first, a tendency to pinch the muscles instead of lifting and working them with the fingers and thumbs. The action is the same as that for kneading dough. It can be used on all muscle groups where you can get a good grip, such as the calves, thighs, hips, back, stomach and chest.

Kneading is performed both along and across the muscles, with the same easy, even rhythm used for the other techniques described. Try to get a good hold of the muscles without pinching them. After completing the initial stage, knead with the palm of the hand in circular movements all along the muscles.

Tapotement
The massage session concludes with vibration of the muscles. Sometimes slapping or "chopping" is used at this time. However, for sporting muscles and muscles in general, all that is needed is vibration or a slight shake of the muscle between thumb and fingers until the desired result is achieved. Slapping and "chopping" do more harm than good and I recommend that you always conclude with vibration and shaking.

Special Equipment

There are several different massage machines on the market, but in my opinion these are not effective. Rather, it is the sensitivity of the masseur's hands that make the massage a success. I do use a vibrator at the end of a session, since it feels pleasant for the subject, but none of the massage machines has any deep-down effect.

Ultrasonic equipment has also become popular, although we don't know what purpose it fulfills. As yet its effects have not been scientifically tested.

I cannot therefore recommend any special equipment aside from vibrators. These are available in most countries. Remember, however, that your hands are the finest pieces of equipment you have available to you. Train them to work sensitively—this takes practice, but they will in time be able to locate the areas of muscular pain and discomfort. And that is the art of massage.

Massaging Different Muscle Groups

The Foot Muscles

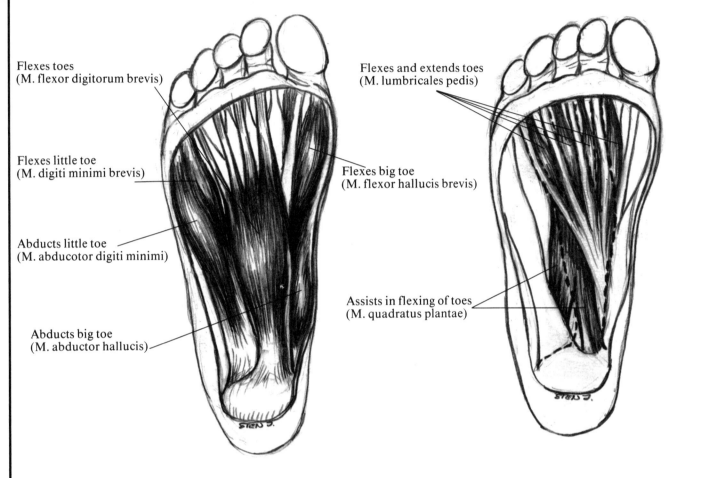

Figure 1
The subject lies on his stomach with his shin supported. In this position the muscles are relaxed and the foot free to be worked on. Begin by smoothing liniment or ointment over and under the foot. Following the illustration, massage each toe in turn. Support the foot with your free hand.
Start first by stroking along the length of the toes and then using circular movements along the length and edges of the toes. Conclude by stretching the toes slightly so that they are properly straightened.

Notes

Figure 2
Hold the foot with both hands and work with the thumbs in the direction of the arrow. Or, you can support the foot with one hand and massage with the thumb of the other, alternating hands to suit yourself. Work all the way down to the heel in this fashion, with both long and outward circular movements of the thumbs. A clenched fist can also be used, applying pressure firmly with the knuckles while supporting the foot steadily with the free hand.

Notes

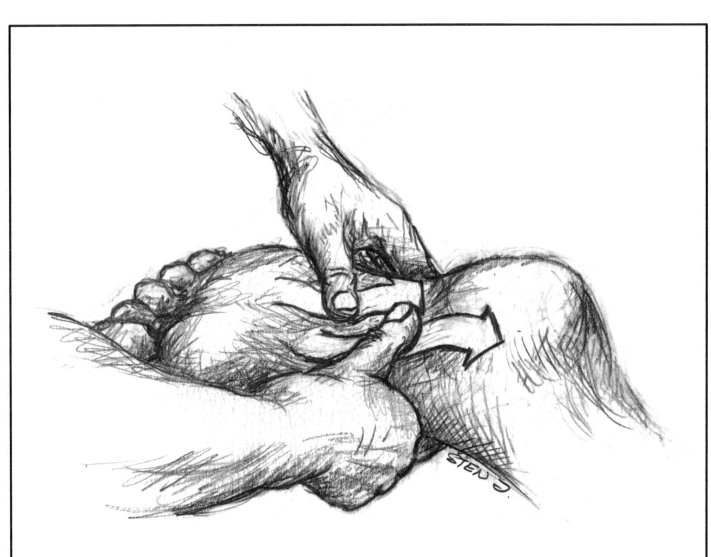

Figure 3
When massaging the foot, the thumbs should follow the direction of the arrows as illustrated in Figure 3. Some subjects find that this tickles, but this sensation can be avoided by applying more pressure. Massaging the instep can produce pain, since waste products often accumulate in these muscles. The same is true of the edges of the foot. In this case, the main joint of the first finger can be used, as in the illustration.

Notes

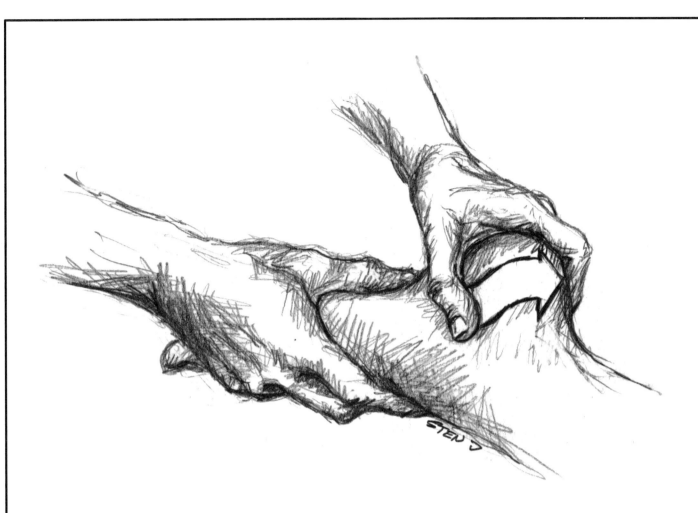

Figure 4
When massaging the heel, begin with the inside, then change hands and massage the outside. Grip the heel and use the whole of the thumb. Support the foot firmly with the free hand, as in the illustration.

Notes

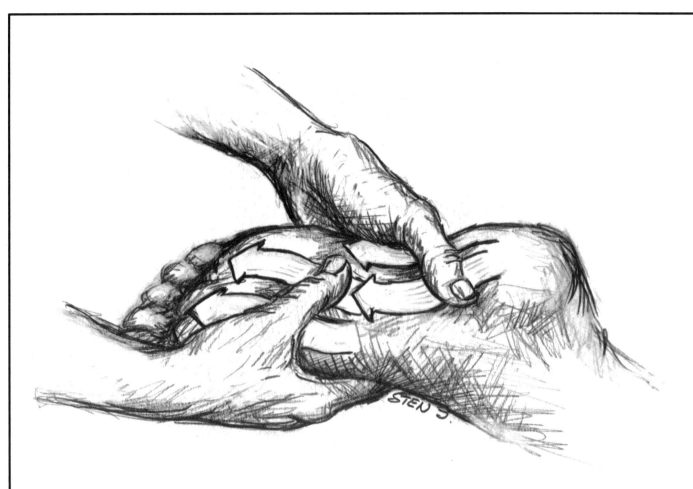

Figure 5
Foot massage concludes with stretching. Stretch the foot lightly to begin with, then somewhat harder 3 or 4 times. Be gentle so that the subject feels relaxed after the massage.

Notes

The Shin Muscles (Front)

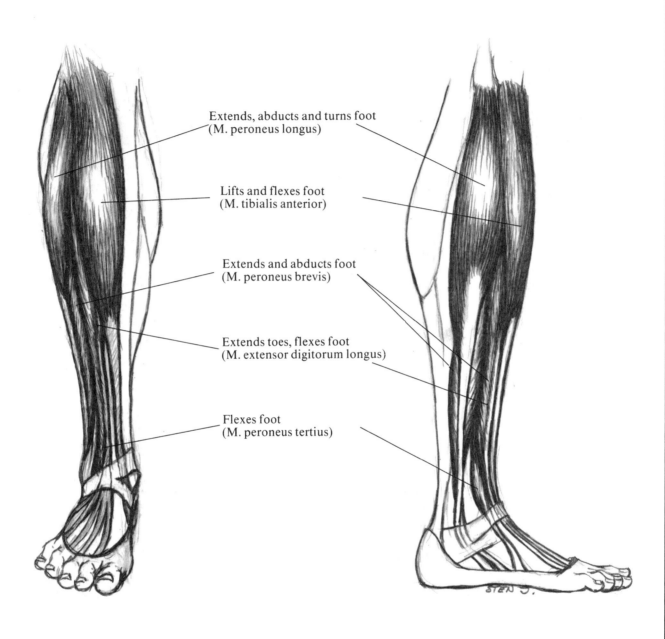

The Shin Muscles (Back)

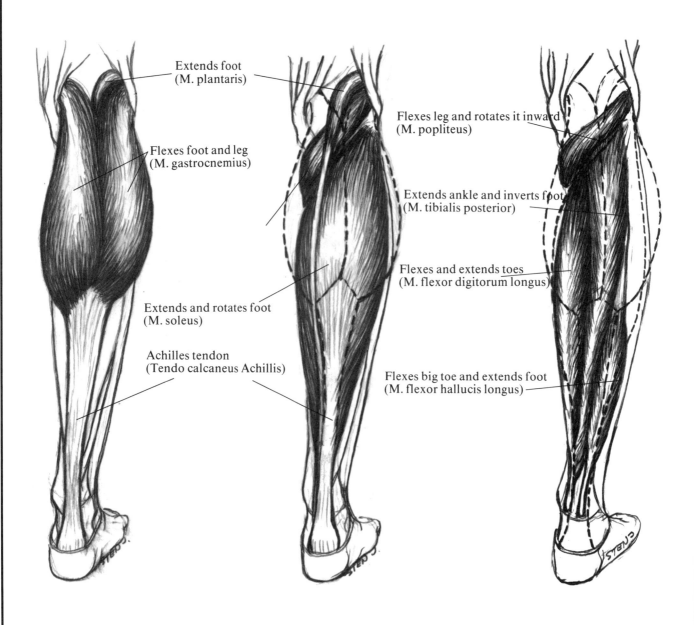

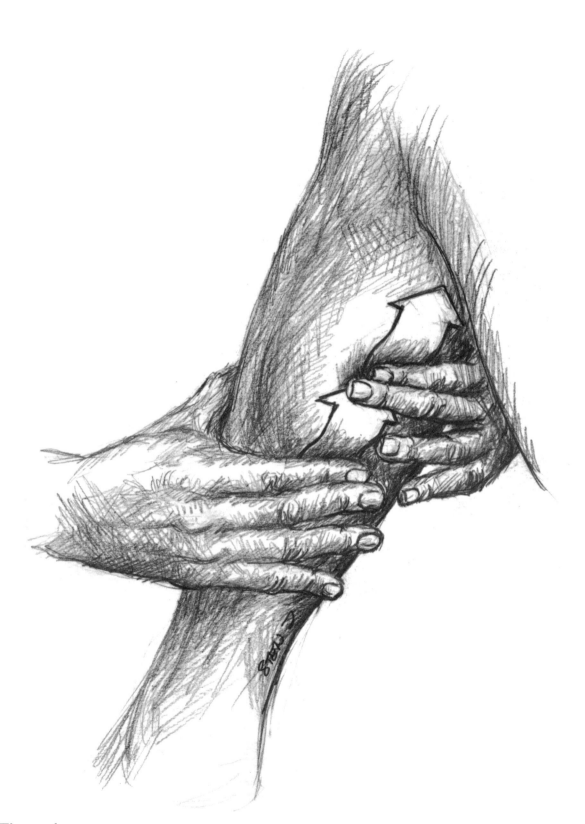

Figure 1
Begin from the point where the Achilles tendon joins the muscles and use all four fingers. Make sure that there is plenty of liniment on the skin so that the fingers glide easily. The right-hand thumb follows the toe extensors while the left-hand thumb glides lightly over the edge of the skin without exerting any pressure. Work for about five minutes in this fashion until the muscles are supple. If the muscles are stiff, it may be necessary to work with them for several sessions in order to free them of waste products.

Notes

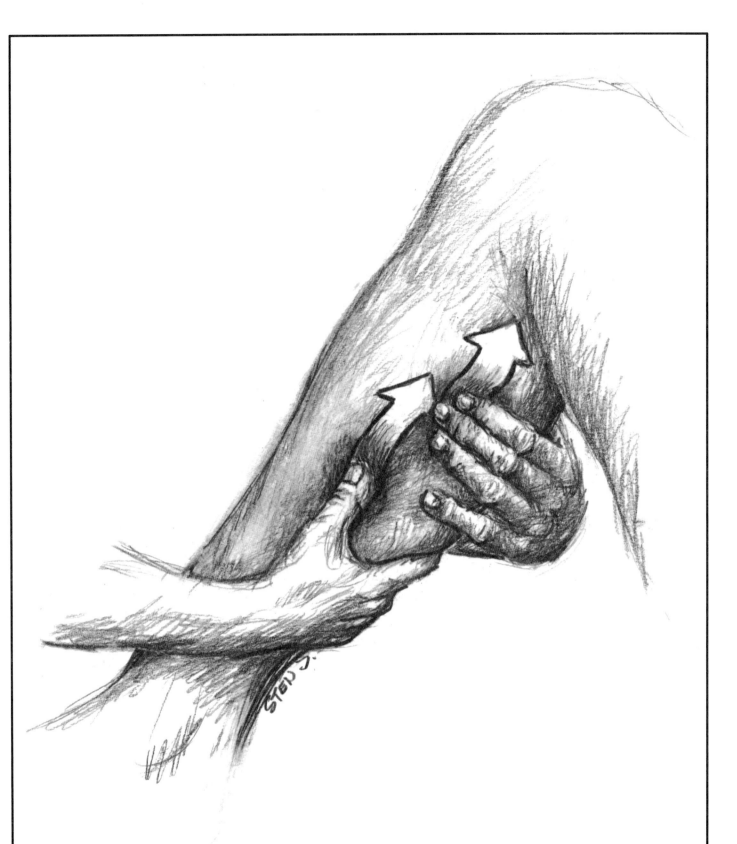

Figure 2
Grip the muscles firmly, so that the thumbs lie deep behind the fibula and shin bones, as in the illustration. Stretch the muscles fully at least 5 or 6 times. Repeat this massage for several minutes before proceeding to Figure 3.

Notes

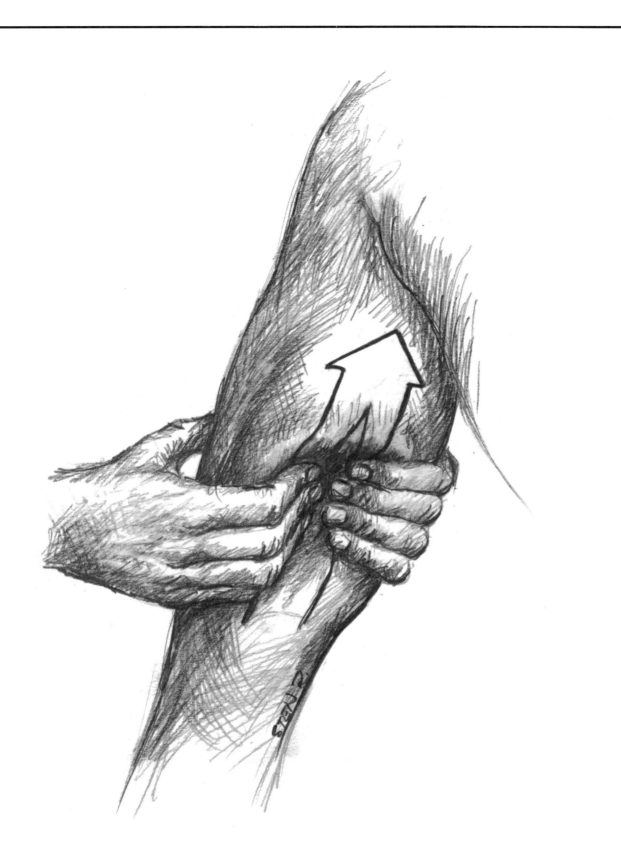

Figure 3
Place the fingers in the middle of the calf so that they divide the double calf muscle (gastrocnemius). The thumbs follow the edges of the fibula and shin bone, the right thumb on the toe extensors. Feel the muscles to be sure that they are supple throughout and free from waste products. If this is not the case, repeat the massages illustrated in Figures 1 and 2 and be sure that the muscles are supple before continuing with Figure 4.

Notes

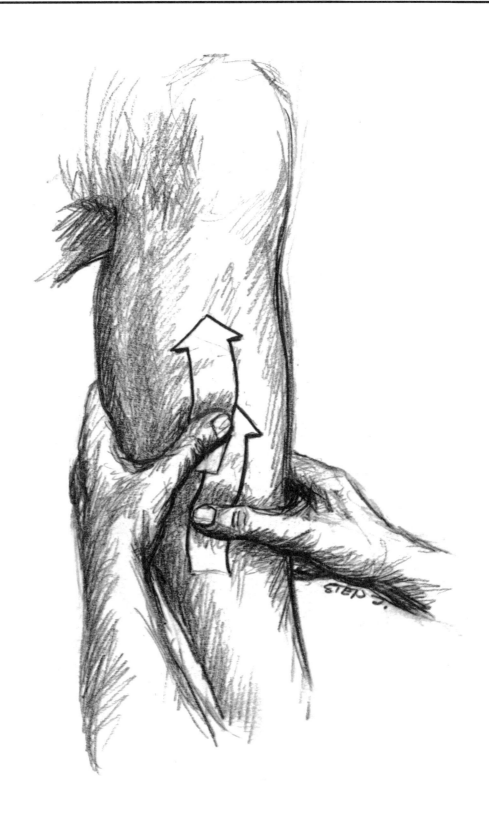

Figure 4
This shows how to massage the toe extensors. It is performed at the same time as the massage illustrated in Figure 1. Work from the ankle and up to the knee. You will now be able to feel that the muscles have become elastic and easier to work with. Finish by vibrating the muscles several times, shaking them lightly between the thumb and fingers.

Notes

The Thigh Muscles (Front)

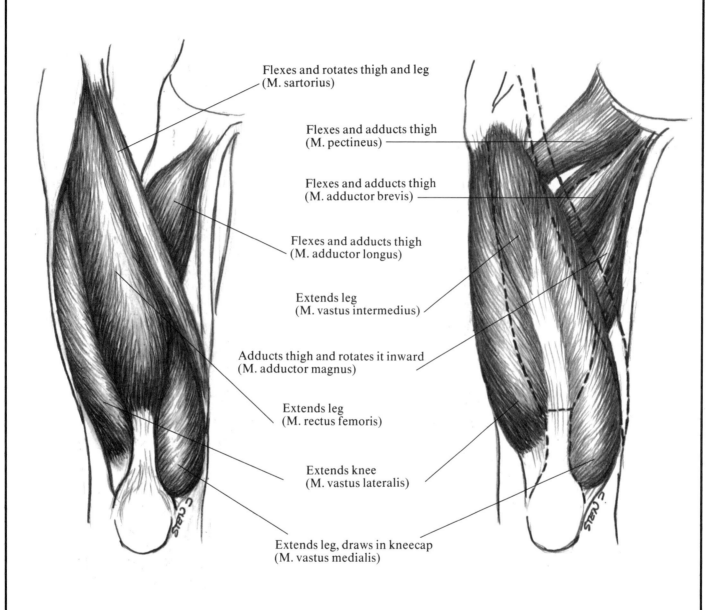

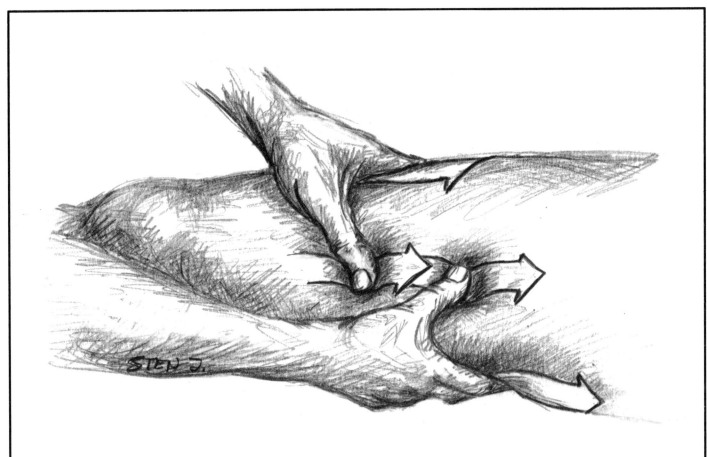

Figure 1
Work with both hands, with thumbs on the front of the thighs and fingers along the sides. Work upwards, towards the heart, as illustrated. Do not use too much pressure in the groin, since there are many glands in this region which do not need massaging. This area can wait until you have acquired greater sensitivity and expertise.

Notes

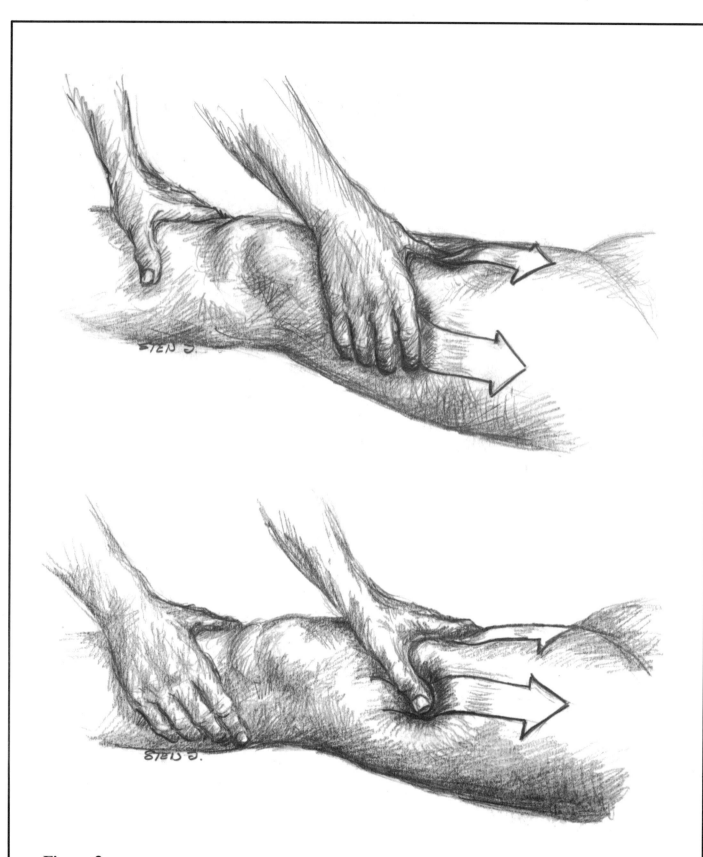

Figure 2
Alternate single-handed massage as illustrated. Hold the arm straight so that you can apply sufficient pressure. Power and body weight of the masseur should be concentrated to his arms.

Notes

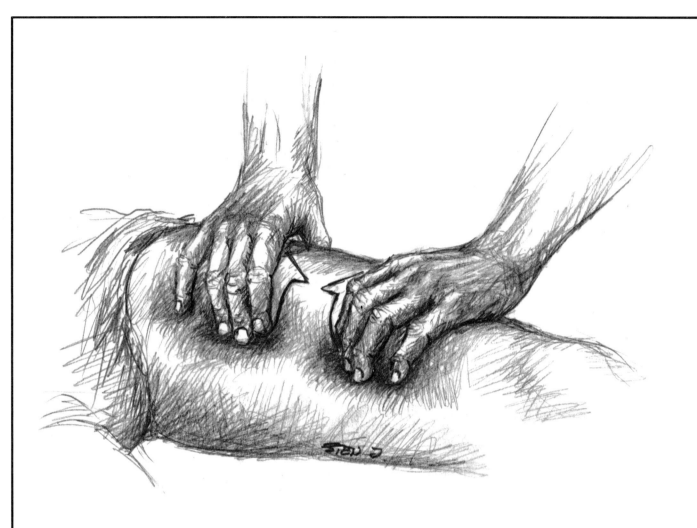

Figure 3
Knead and lift the thigh muscles according to the directions given for this technique on page 13. Try to grasp the muscles as illustrated, lifting and stretching them. Follow this by kneading the muscles with circular movements and repeat the entire procedure several times.

Notes

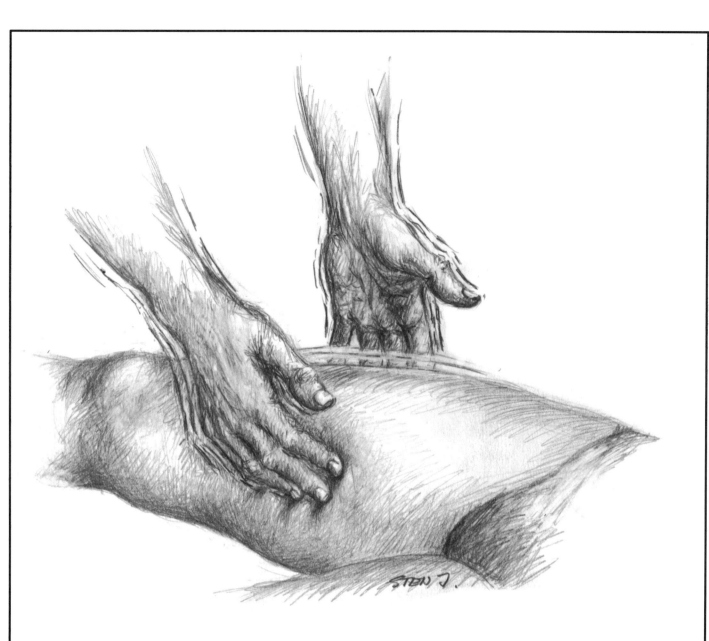

Figure 4
Massage of each muscle group concludes with vibration with the fingers as shown, the palms of the hands facing each other. The muscles are not to be slapped, simply vibrated.

Notes

The Thigh Muscles (Back)

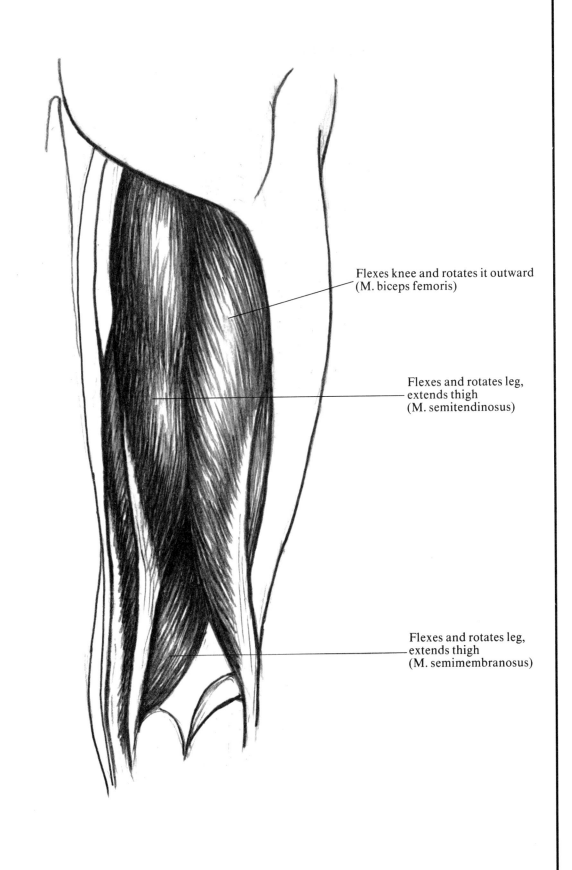

Flexes knee and rotates it outward (M. biceps femoris)

Flexes and rotates leg, extends thigh (M. semitendinosus)

Flexes and rotates leg, extends thigh (M. semimembranosus)

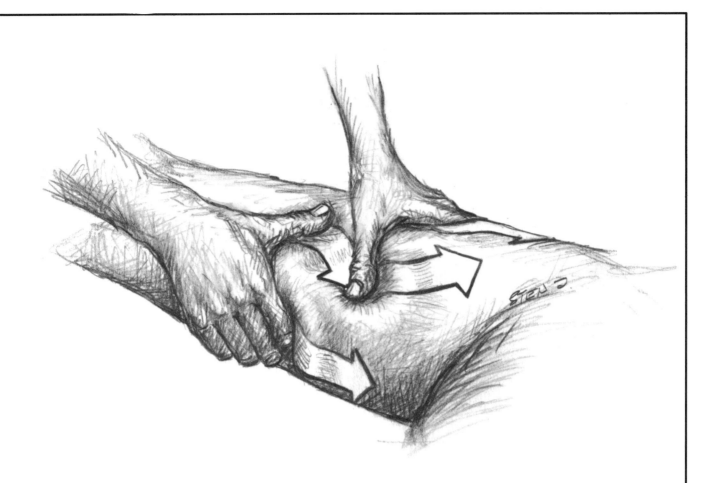

Figure 1
Massage and loosen the muscles with both hands as illustrated, beginning about 4 inches above the knee joint. Do not massage the knee itself as it is difficult to avoid putting pressure on the bursa, causing irritation.

Notes

Figure 2
Increase the pressure using single-handed massage. Alternate hands so that both sides of the thighs are massaged. Massage all the way up to the buttocks.

Notes

54

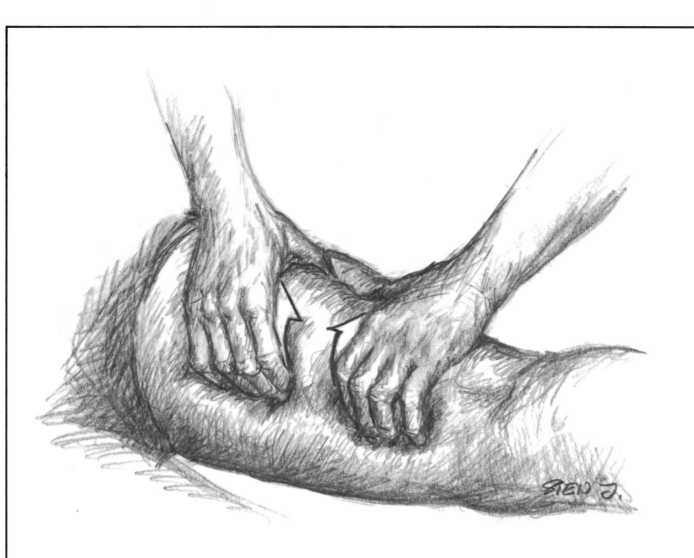

Figure 3
After massaging the muscles as described in Figures 1—2, begin kneading and lifting. Knead the muscles quite firmly before beginning to lift and stretch them. Conclude by vibrating the muscles lightly between fingers and thumb.

Notes

The Hip Muscles

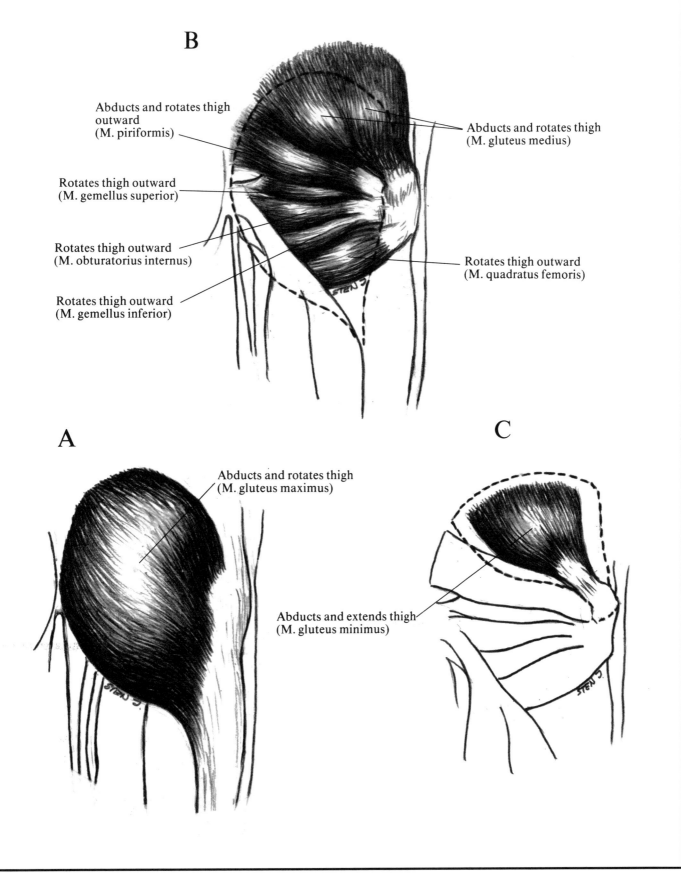

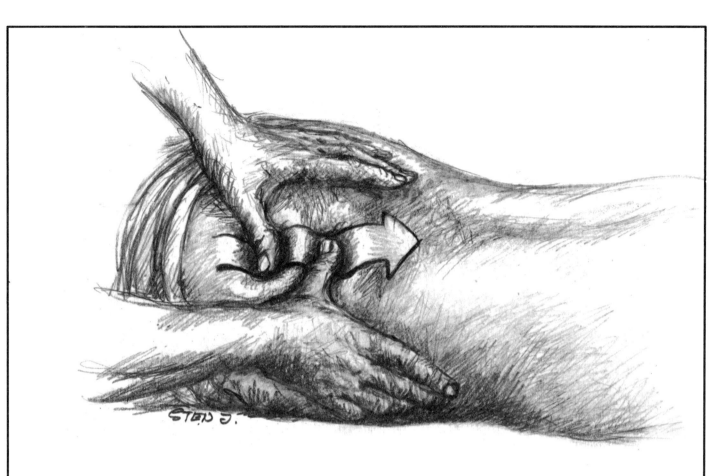

Figure 1
Begin by warming up the buttock muscles as shown. Massage from the rump bone each muscle and up over the entire hip section. These muscles are often stiff and sore and it is therefore best to begin superficially, gradually massaging deeper and deeper. The massage should not be painful. It is worth devoting considerable time to these muscles as they are the origin of many cases of lumbago.

Notes

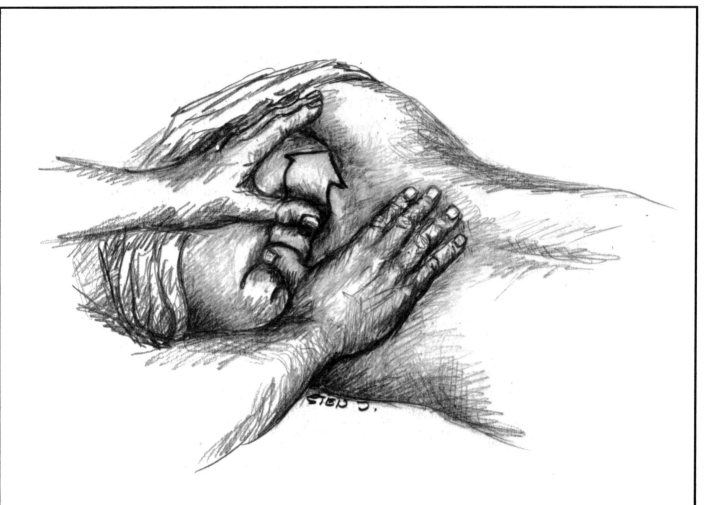

Figure 2
Change the direction of massage and work from the sides towards the crotch. Considerable pressure can be used. You should work hard with your thumbs, as shown in the illustration—almost as if kneading.

Notes

The Superficial Back Muscles

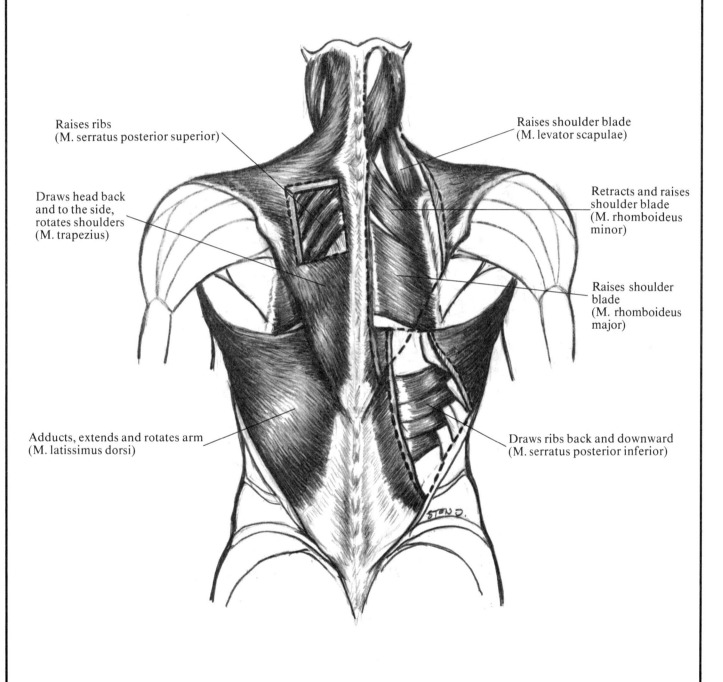

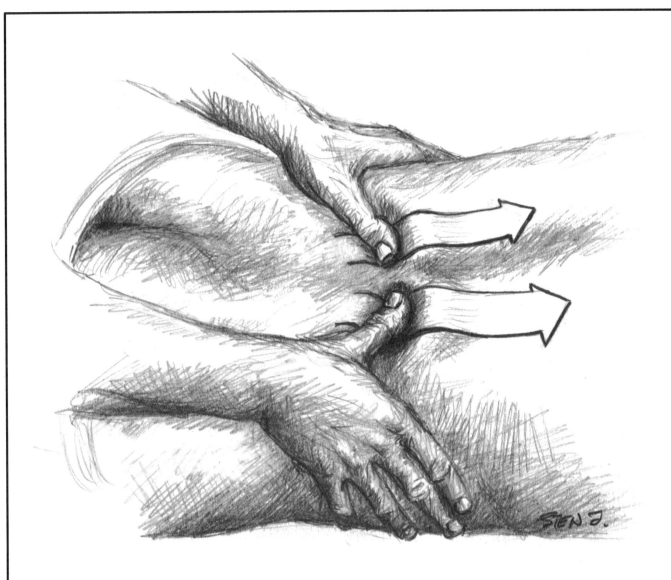

Figure 1
When finished with the hips, move on to the broad back muscles. Work with the thumbs: upwards, outwards and toward the shoulders. Begin from the lower spine and proceed along the entire muscle system of the back.

Notes

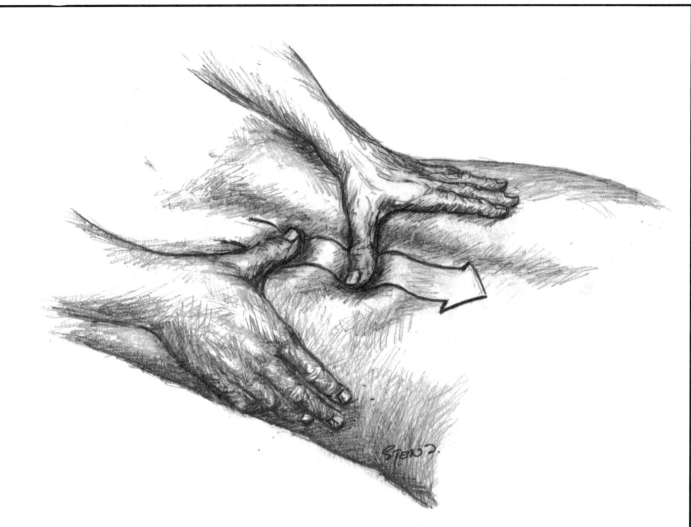

Figure 2
Now massage across the muscles of the back, from the hips up to the shoulders.

Notes

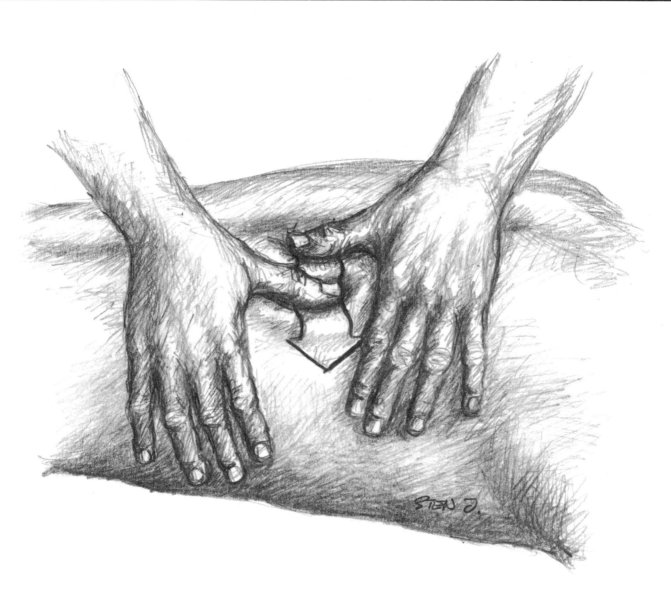

Figure 3
So as to increase the pressure, work with both hands or thumbs in sequence as illustrated, all the way from the base of the spine up to the shoulders. Alternate sides as the muscles become supple.

Notes

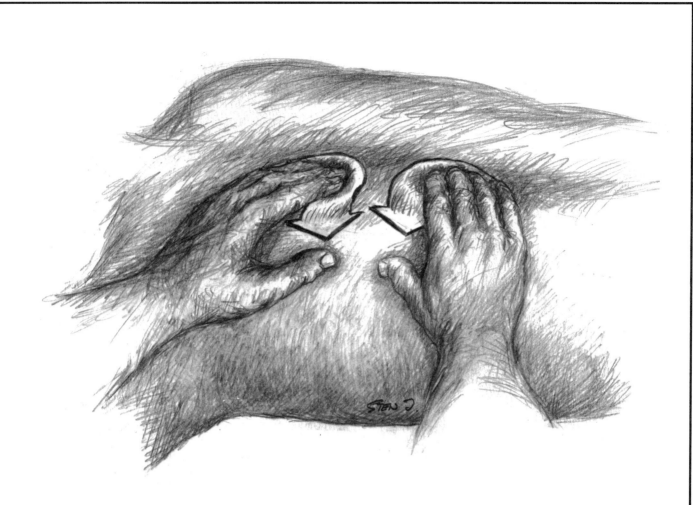

Figure 4
The back muscles should then be kneaded, using a circular movement. Press firmly with the fingers using the thumbs for support. Try to grasp the muscles so that each group, around the armpit and shoulders and from the spine outwards, is thoroughly worked on. Repeat this massage pattern several times.

Notes

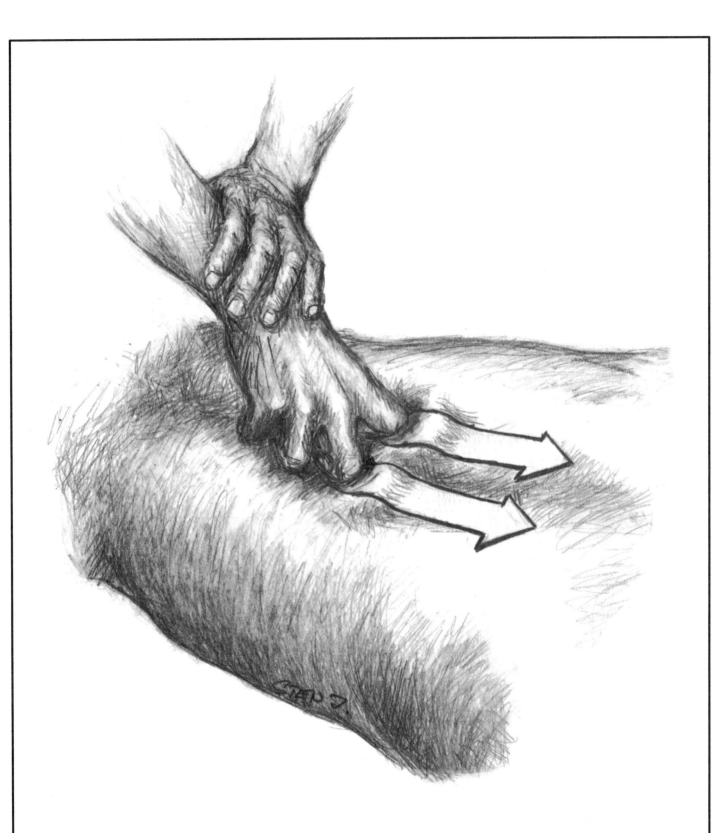

Figure 5
Before concluding the back massage, push with the knuckles along the edges of the spine, from the waist up to the neck. Do this very firmly several times, without pressing on the spine itself. Finally, place your hands on the subject's hips and vibrate by rotating the hands with a light pressure all the way up to the neck, until you feel that all the muscles are relaxed and supple.

Notes

The Shoulder Muscles

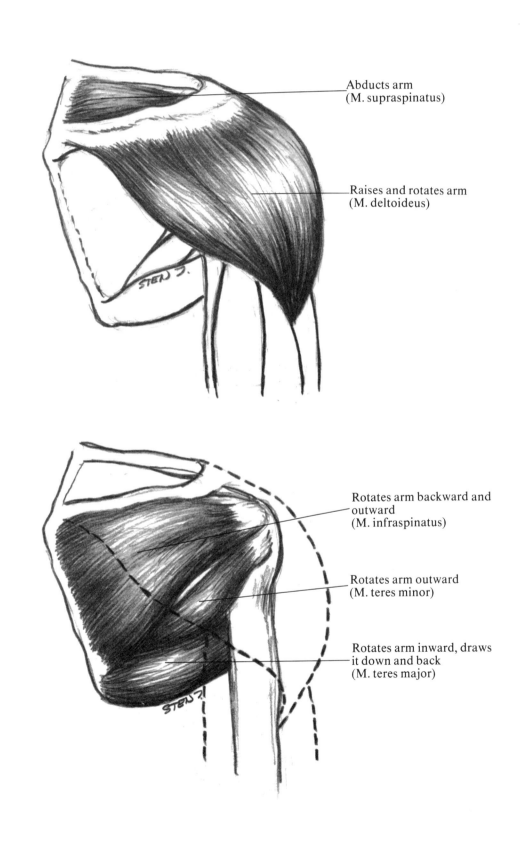

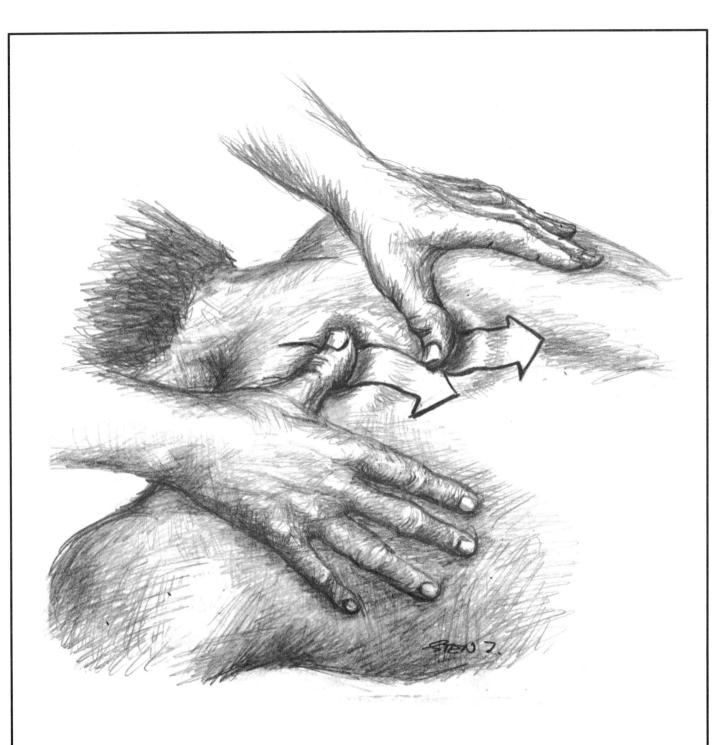

Figure 1
Begin at the neck and work with both hands, as illustrated, massaging between the shoulders. Let the subject place his arms beside his body so as to increase the area between the shoulder and the spine. Continue massaging as shown in the illustration.

Notes

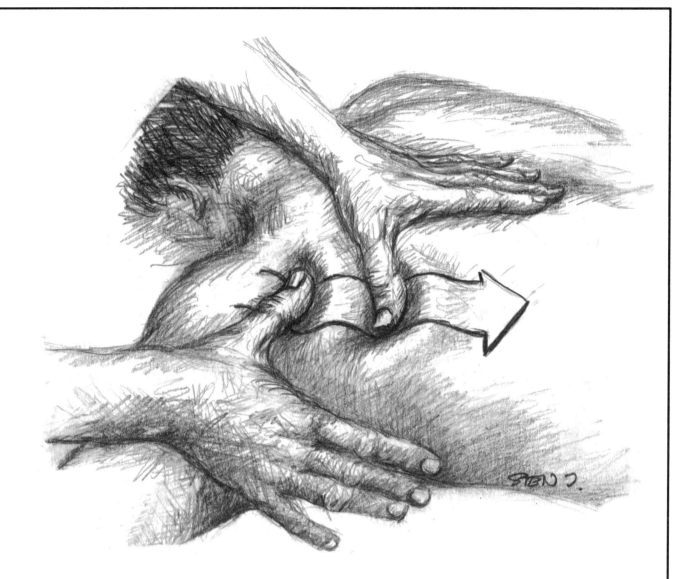

Figure 2
Massaging with one thumb and then the other, as shown in the illustration, will bring effective relief to stiff shoulder muscles.

Notes

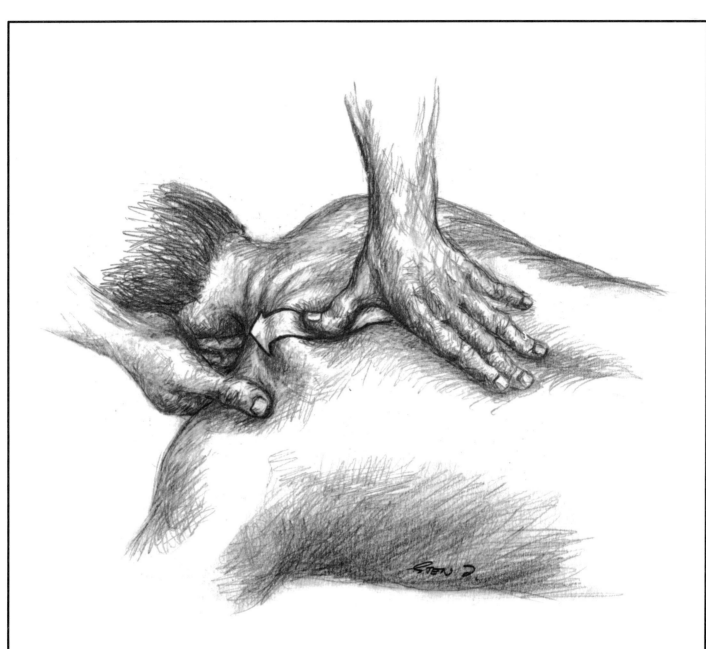

Figure 3
Let the subject's arm hang free from the massage table. Place the fingers lightly on the muscles below the shoulder and work with the thumbs as shown. Firm pressure can be applied.

Notes

The Neck Muscles

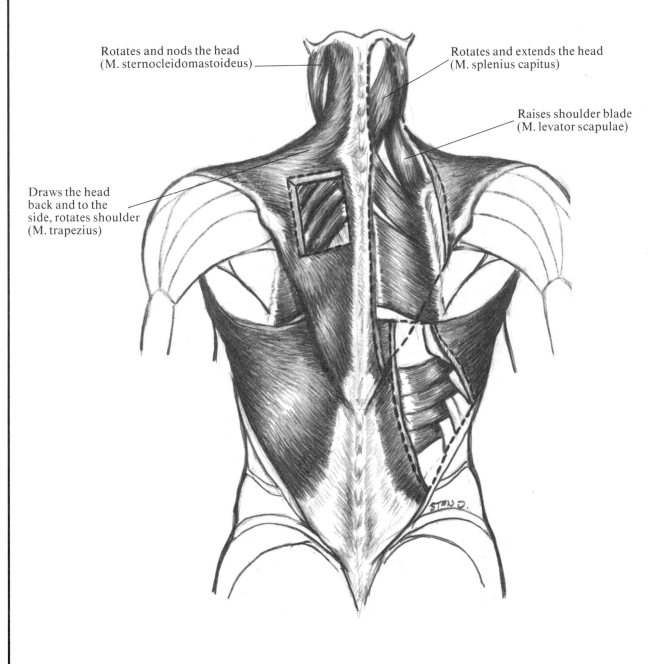

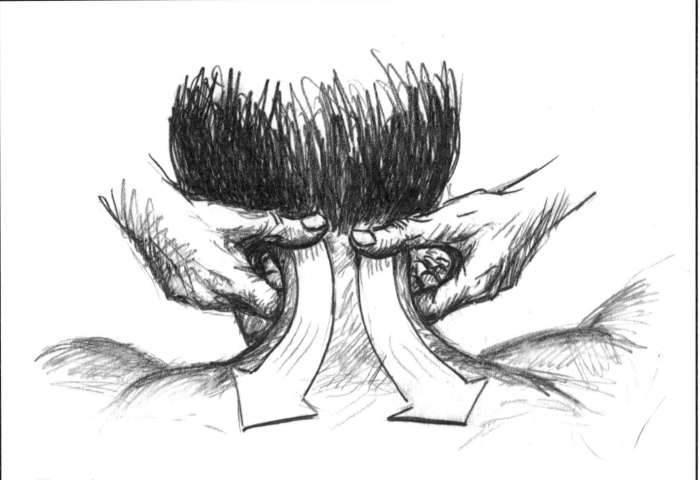

Figure 1

Begin working with the thumbs downwards from the base of the skull, as illustrated. Support the muscles with the index fingers, allowing the thumbs to work freely. Do not press too firmly with the fingers against the throat — use them simply for support and to lift the muscles upwards as shown in the illustration.

Notes

Figure 2
Continue working with the muscles around the base of the neck and down towards the shoulders. Here again, the fingers are used to lift the muscles. Feel for the collarbone and use the index finger to support the muscles while the thumbs are working freely. Complete the massage of one side of the neck before switching to the other. Finally, take hold of the neck muscles and lift them up, as if plucking them. Do the same with the shoulder muscles.

Notes

The Superficial Forearm Extensors

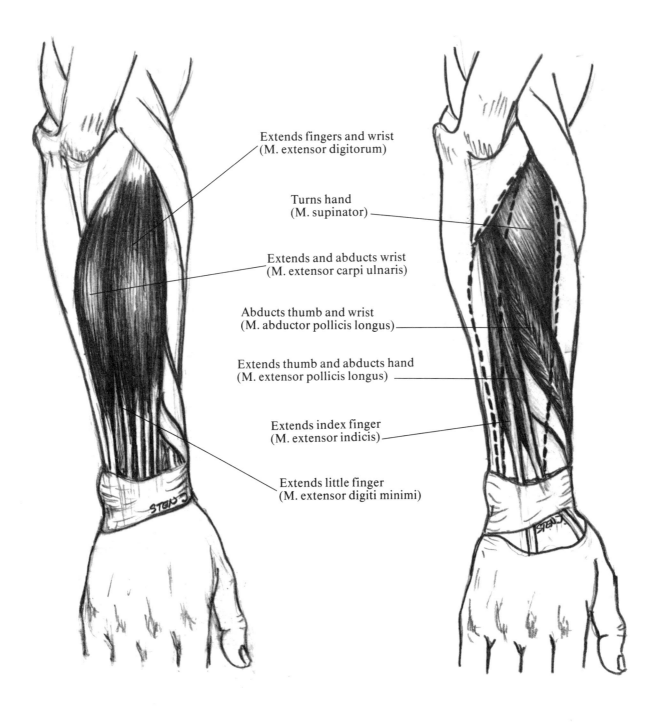

The Superficial Forearm Flexors

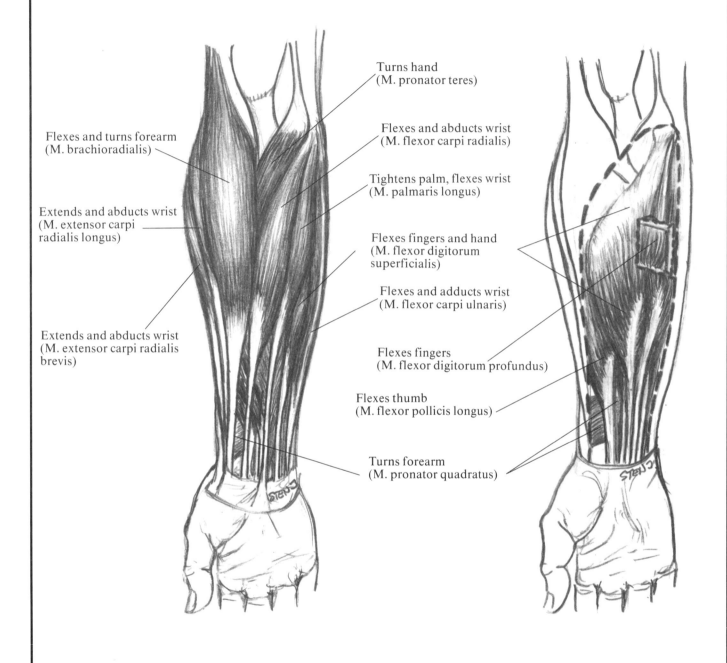

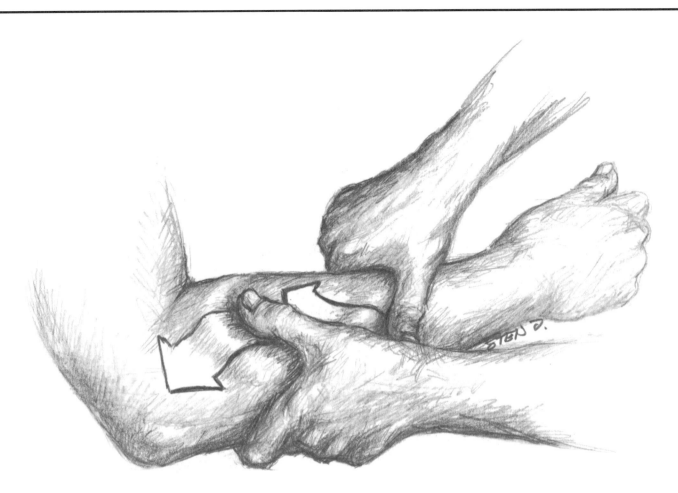

Figure 1
Begin with the forearm as shown in the illustration. The best results are obtained by holding the arm on the massage table and working with the thumbs, using circular movements. The Fingers work on the inside of the arm along the muscles. The grip goes around the entire forearm. The muscles should be supple before going on to the next step.

Notes

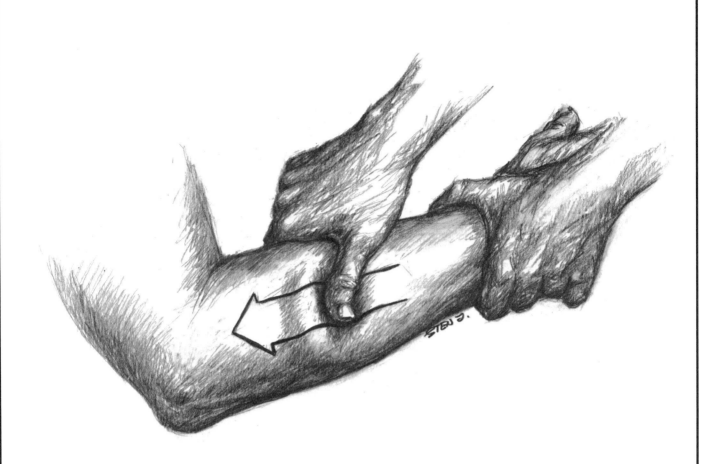

Figure 2
Change the grip so that you reach all the muscles on the outside of the arm. Begin from the wrist and work towards the elbow. Brace your fingers so that you get a good grip on the muscles.

Notes

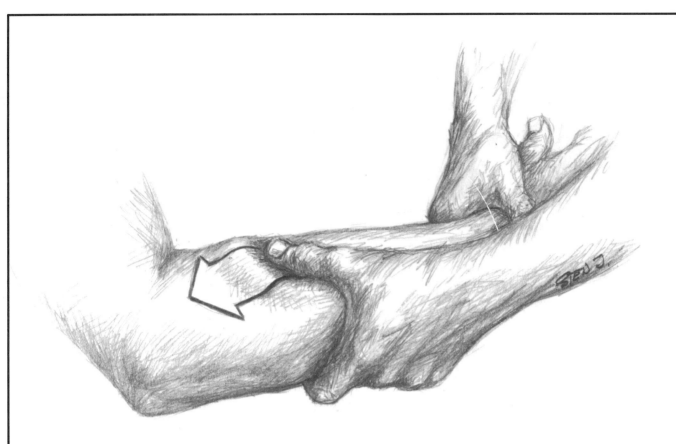

Figure 3
Hold the wrist lightly and press with the thumb on the inside of the forearm and the fingers on the outside of the forearm. Begin by pressing lightly with the thumb and then increase the pressure. But be careful, because the muscles on the outside of the forearm—the extensors—can be painful if too much pressure is applied.

Notes

The Upper Arm Muscles (Front)

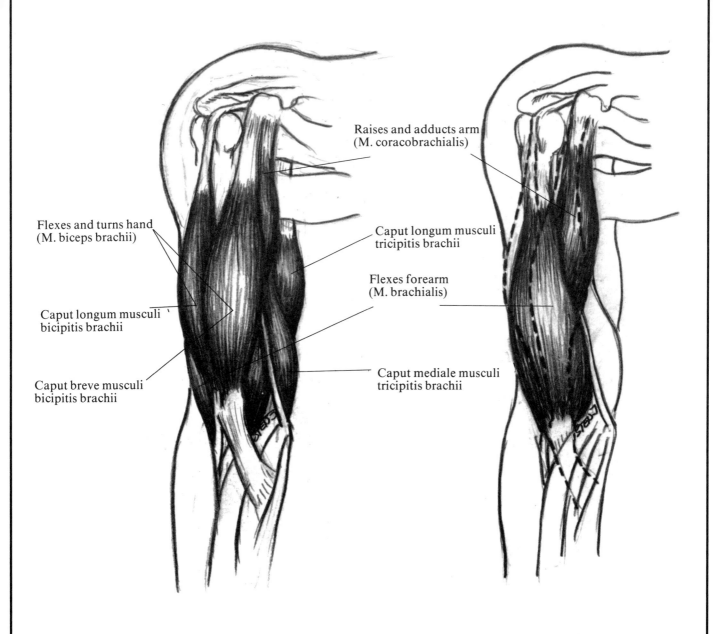

The Upper Arm Muscles (Back)

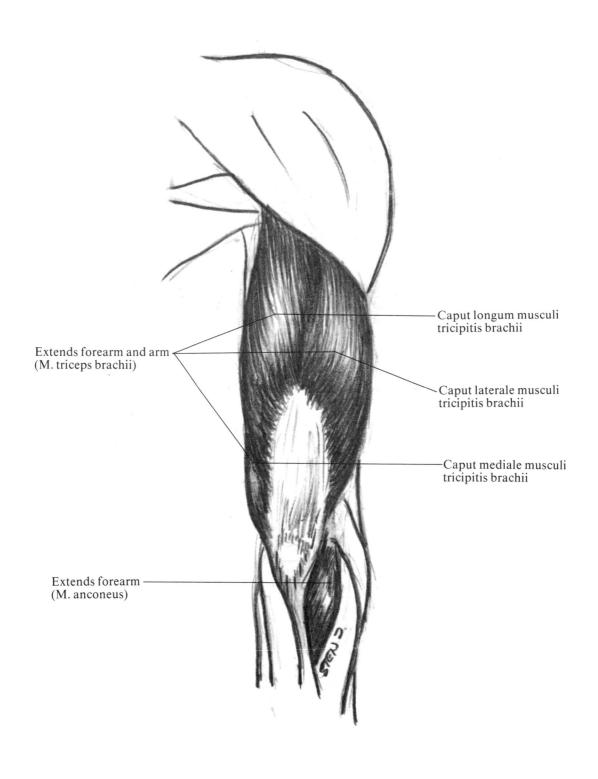

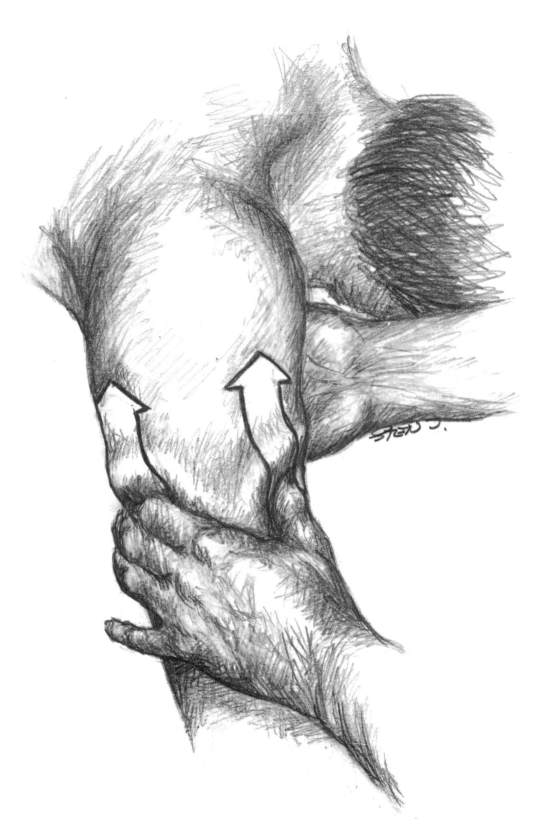

Figure 1
In the upper arm, only the biceps and triceps need massage. Keep your free hand under the upperarm for improved grip and support. Work with the thumb and fingers around the muscles as illustrated.

Notes

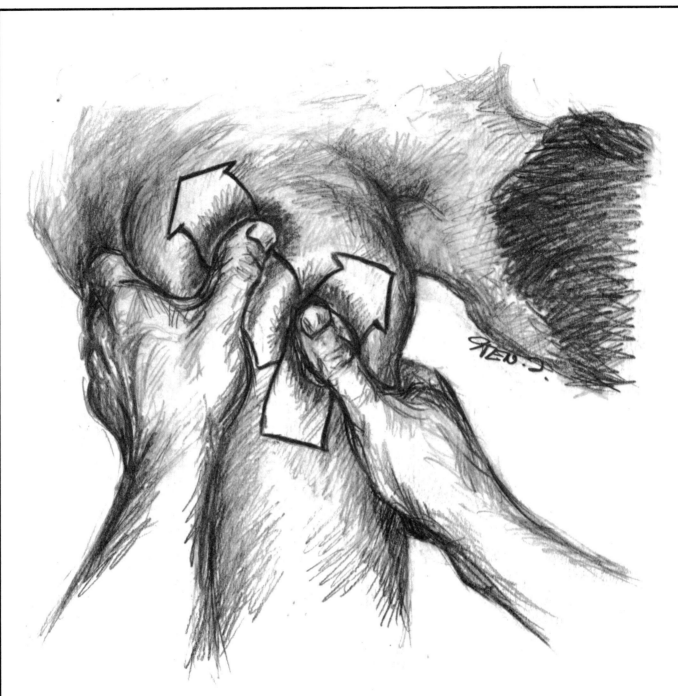

Figure 2
This time the fingers are placed just at the edge of the armpits. It is easy to feel the upper arm muscles. Work all the way up from the elbow to the shoulder. Work separately on the biceps and triceps. Lift them in turn and massage by stroking so that they receive thorough treatment.

Notes

The Stomach Muscles

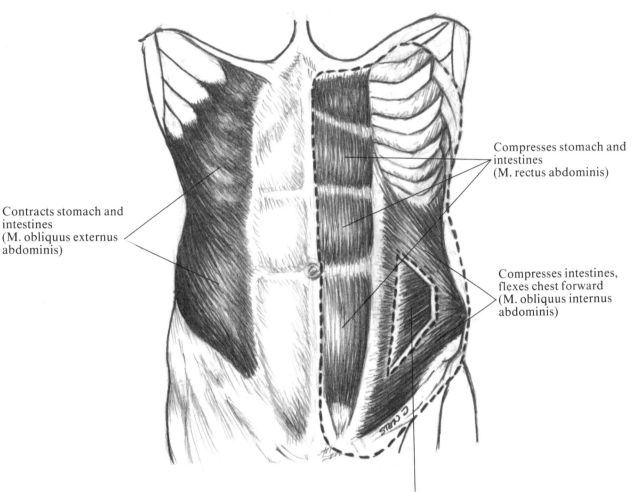

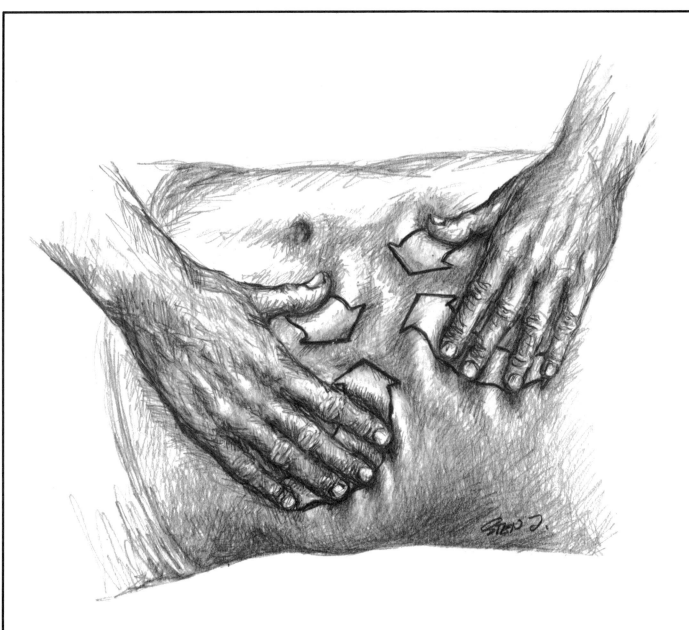

Figure 1
Massage the stomach muscles and sides of the stomach as illustrated. Work along the stomach muscles first for 2 to 3 minutes, and then continue up to the ribs and chest cavity.

Notes

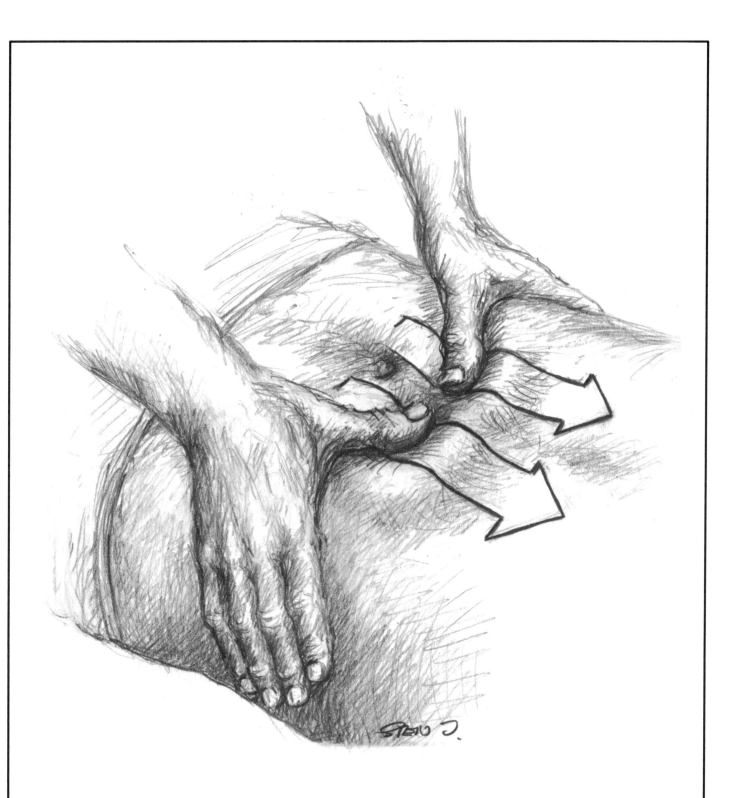

Figure 2
Massage across the muscles with fingers and thumbs as illustrated. Begin from the hips and continue up to the ribs. Work carefully, without pressing too hard. Continue in this fashion until you reach the chest cavity and breastbone.

Notes

The Superficial Chest Muscles

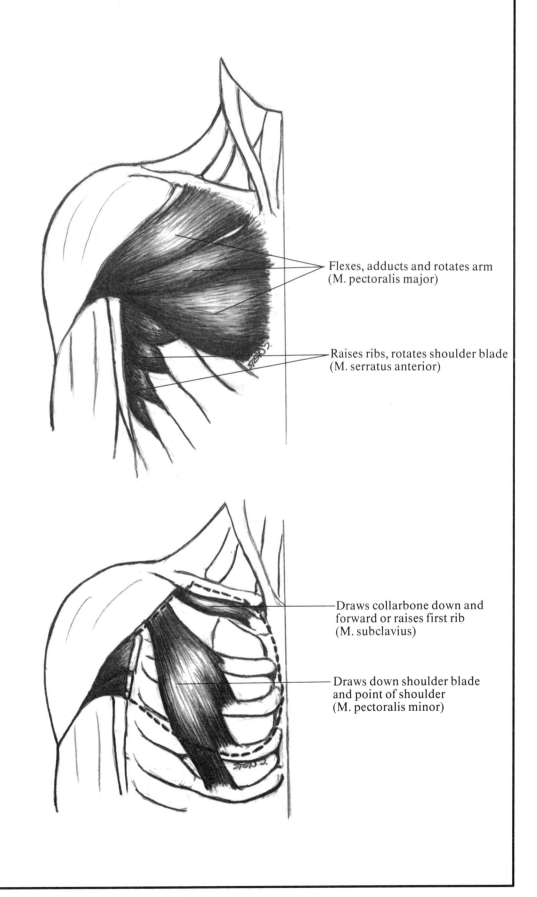

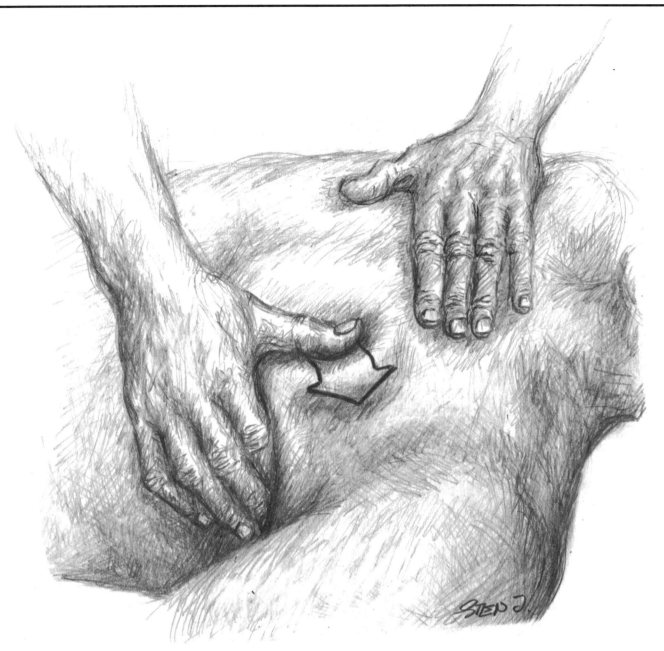

Figure 1
The chest can be massaged either with each hand alternately as in the illustration, or slowly with both hands. Do not press too hard on and around the shoulder joint. Here there are no muscles but bursae which can be irritated by hard pressure. It is easy to feel where the chest muscles lie—concentrate your massage on them!

Notes

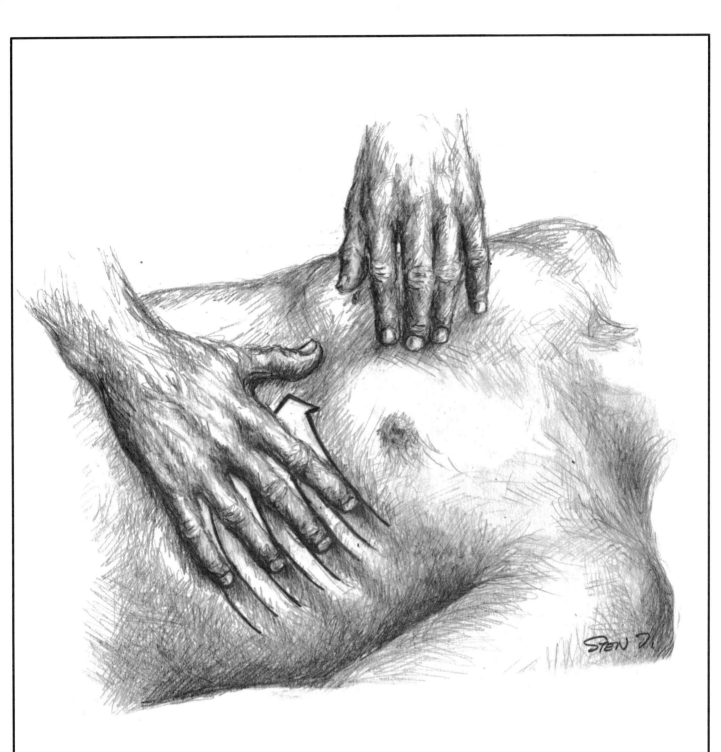

Figure 2
The muscles around the ribs are often stiff and should be massaged with care. These muscles are very important for breathing. As mentioned previously, do not press too hard. Use a soft, light touch so that the subject can enjoy the massage. Ask him to breath deeply, in and out, so you can feel the elasticity of the muscles.

Notes

Some Final Tips

Foot Massage

Try to support the foot firmly with the free hand when massaging the toes. Work with a calm and even rhythm. If the subject is ticklish, it usually helps to massage more firmly, although pressure should never be excessive.

Shin Massage

Use plenty of liniment or massage ointment, particularly if the subject is hairy where he or she is to be massaged. It is easy to irritate the hair follicles, causing itching and discomfort which can last several days. Look carefully at the illustrations showing the different stages of massage; do not pinch, but work smoothly and rhythmically. Take plenty of time—you can never achieve good results by rushing a massage. Do not press too hard on the edges of the bones. The thumb should just be able to feel the shin-bone.

Thigh Massage

The front of the thigh is massaged from the knee and upwards towards the groin. Do not, however, massage the lymph gland and other small glands in the groin. Apply liniment or ointment generously, not only to the fronts of the thighs but to the insides, which should be massaged before proceeding to the backs. Begin massaging the backs of the thighs about 4 inches above the knee. Avoid the knee joint since the bursa—a pocket of fibrous tissue—can be da-maged if pressure is put on it. This is true of other joints as well, so that joints in general should be left alone.

Hip Massage

The hips are massaged from the rump bone and up over the buttocks, from the sides and towards the crotch. Look at the illustrations showing the direction of the hip muscles and follow these.

Do not press down too hard, but allow the thumbs to move as illustrated. Too much pressure will produce bruising, making it uncomfortable for the subject to sit down for several days. This is not the purpose of the exercise! Remember that all massage should be gentle initially until the muscles have adjusted themselves to the treatment.

Back Massage

Back massage covers a large section of the body, from the hips up to the shoulders. The job will be easier if you follow the different stages illustrated. Massage with an even rhythm and a light touch to begin with and then increase the pressure as directed by the subject. Always ask if the pressure is right—this way you will gain valuable experience. Do not massage the spinal column. All circular massage movements should begin from the spine and move outwards. Remember to stroke the muscles between the ribs using the fingers, as you would for chest massage.

Shoulder Massage

There are many different muscles in the shoulder region which you will soon learn to recognize by touch. Work as shown in the illustrations, from the base of the neck outwards and up between the soulder blades. Change hands for each side of the neck, placing the finger above the collarbone for support. This gives greater control over the massage. Lift the muscles simutaneously so that the different stages of the shoulder massage are easier to perform.

When working with the thumb against the neck, the muscles can be treated more satisfactorily if the subject's arms lie next to the body. When massaging the outside of the shoulders, however, it is better if the arms are placed in a forward position. The muscles around the shoulders are often painful. This is usually a result of tension—the pain can be massaged away. Massage will never cause pain in a healthy muscle.

Neck Massage

Many people suffer from headaches that are the result of tension in the neck muscles. Neck massage is therefore important and although this is not a large section of the body, there are many muscles to be massaged. Many of them run down the back, where they are attached. Begin as shown in the illustrations and remember not to put too much pressure on the throat. By and large, it is only the thumbs that are active in neck massage. Finish the massage by lifting the muscles in the neck with the thumbs. The shoulder muscles can also be lifted and stretched in this way.

Arm Massage

The best position for the subject when massaging the arms is lying on the stomach, since that way the arms are relaxed. Begin with both thumbs before switching to alternating, single-handed massage. The arm muscles are easy to feel. Those in the front of the forearm are often painful, so massage initially with a light touch. The upper arm is massaged from the elbow up to the shoulder socket. Use the thumbs as illustrated when massaging the deltoid muscle. Do not apply too much pressure with the fingers under the armpit. The fingers are simply, intended to give support to the grip. There is no need to massage the inside of the arm.

Stomach Massage

The stomach should be massaged lightly and for a few minutes only. Work with the thumb grip as illustrated, using circular movements. Finish by stroking from the pelvis up to the chest cavity. Massage the chest cavity with light, circular movements following the ribs. Conclude by stroking upwards with the palm of the hand. This has the effect of lifting the stomach muscles.

Chest Massage

The chest muscles are massaged with each hand in turn or both together. A large bursa lies in front of the shoulder joint and this should not be massaged. Concentrate instead on massaging between the ribs as shown. Use each hand in turn, but do not press too hard. Massage of the muscles between the ribs makes it easier to expand the rib cage.

General Remarks

It is important to remember the following: begin massaging with a light hand and, gradually, through repeated practice, you will learn to recognize the muscles that build up and support the skeleton. Be sure to avoid causing irritation and tension. Massage should be pleasurable although experience has taught me that it can be painful to begin with. I also know that, with repeated treatment, discomfort will disappear and the muscles will feel firm, supple, and relaxed.

Notes

Notes

Also by Bertil Ravald

GET FIT FOR GOLF

This is a book for all who aim to be fitter and better golf players and who want to enjoy their hobby well into their old age.

We all know that two of the basic qualities of a good golfer are an excellent physique and good coordination, but few of us do anything about it! Strength, stamina and fitness are essential when playing golf and in this book you will find a training program which, with a little effort from you, will work wonders for your game!

Bertil Ravald offers suggestions for a fitness program carried out at home, but which can also be used for group training. He also recommends a warming-up routine that will help reduce tension and create the prerequisites for a perfect stroke, right from the first tee.

The book contains advice on how typical golf injuries can be avoided. And if an injury should occur, you will find expert guidance on how to alleviate it using taping or supportive bandaging. Clear illustrations and diagrams by Sten Johnson show you how such bandaging should be applied.

The Bergh Publishing Group, Inc.

c/o E. P. Dutton – 2 Park Avenue – New York, N.Y. 10016
Telephone: (212) 725-1818